ENERGY SOURCES

Facts · Issues · The Future

BIOMASS POWER

NEIL MORRIS

W

FRANKLIN WATTS
LONDON · SYDNEY

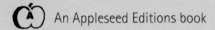 An Appleseed Editions book

First published in 2006 by Franklin Watts

Reprinted 2007

Franklin Watts
338 Euston Road, London NW1 3BH

Franklin Watts Australia
Level 17/207 Kent St, Sydney, NSW 2000

© 2006 Appleseed Editions

Created by Appleseed Editions Ltd, Well House,
Friars Hill, Guestling, East Sussex TN35 4ET

Designed by Guy Callaby
Edited by Mary-Jane Wilkins
Picture research by Su Alexander

ISBN 0 7496 6739 7

Dewey Classification: 333.95'39

A CIP catalogue for this book is available
from the British Library

Photographs by
Front cover: Jean Heguy/Corbis; title page Bill Stormont/Corbis; 4 Bill
Ross/Corbis; 5 H. David Seawell/Corbis; 6 DK Limited/Corbis; 7t George
D. Lepp, b Sylvain Saustier/Corbis; 8 Eric & David Hosking; 9 Graham
Howden; Cordaiy Photo Library Ltd./Corbis; 10 Hans Georg Roth/Corbis;
11t Bill Stormont/Corbis, b Jeffrey L. Rotman/Corbis; 12 Bill Varie/Corbis;
13t Kennan Ward/Corbis, b M.Fife/ZEFA; 14 Paulo Whitaker/Reuters/
Corbis; 15 Vo Trung Dung/Corbis Sygma; 16 Prof. David Hall/Science
Photo Library; 17 Louie Psihoyos/Corbis; 18 Russ Schleipman/Corbis;
19t Earl & Nazima Kowall/Corbis, b Roger Ressmeyer/Corbis; 20 Ferdaus
Shamim/Corbis; 21 Olaf Gallas/General Motors/Reuters/Corbis; 22 Liba
Taylor/Corbis; 23t Vince Streano/Corbis, b Peter Guttman/Corbis;
24 Chris Knapton/Science Photo Library; 25 Christine Osborne/Corbis;
26 Owen Franken/Corbis; 27 Galen Rowell/Corbis; 28 Layne Kennedy/
Corbis; 29t Elsam Kraft, b Tom Brakefield/Corbis;

Printed in China

Franklin Watts is a division
of Hachette Children's Books

Contents

The world of living things

People have burned wood, other plants and animal wastes for hundreds of thousands of years. They have always been useful fuels for heating and cooking. Scientists call all plant and animal matter biomass, which combines the Greek word *bios* (meaning life) with *mass* (meaning quantity of matter).

The world's forests are the largest source of plant matter, in the form of trees. They provide wood, which we use as building material, for making paper and as a fuel.

In recent times we have learned to use biomass as an energy source to power machines. The term energy also comes from a Greek word, *energos*, which means active or working. Energy sources help other things become active and do work, such as lifting or moving objects. For example, biomass power – or bioenergy – can be used to make electricity. So when you switch on a light in your home, the energy to make it work might have come from biomass.

Storing solar energy

We live on a solar-powered planet, and the Sun is the source of the energy that exists in biomass. All the world's plants and animals need the power of the Sun's rays to survive. Plants change the Sun's rays into chemical energy, which they are able to store and use to live. This means that the world's biomass is really a store of solar energy.

Natural process

If people did not use biomass to produce energy, it would give off heat naturally as it decomposed. By using biomass we are speeding up a natural process, and we can plant more trees – or other plants – to replace those we use to produce energy. This is why biomass is a renewable resource. However, it is different from other renewable sources, because as we use it, we need to make sure that it is properly replaced.

RENEWABLE RESOURCE

Biomass is called a renewable resource, because it can be replaced and should never run out. This is different from some other energy sources, such as coal and oil, which take millions of years to form and are non-renewable. Geothermal, solar, water and wind power are also renewable forms of energy.

The Sun is the Earth's ultimate energy source.

Producers of food and energy

The world's biomass is made up of plants and animals living in many different habitats. Groups of living things interact with each other and form communities. Each community and its environment of non-living things, such as rocks, soil and water, form an ecosystem.

The Sun is the original source of energy for all the Earth's ecosystems. Scientists call plants producers, because they use the Sun's energy to produce food. They do this by soaking up sunlight in their leaves and using it to combine carbon dioxide gas from the air with water from the soil. This combining process, called photosynthesis, helps plants make their own sugary food. At the same time, they give off oxygen, which other living things (including humans) need to breathe and stay alive.

This glass case is called a terrarium. It is like a home-made ecosystem, with its own soil, plants, animals and atmosphere.

Energy flow

While plants are producers, the animals in an ecosystem are consumers. Primary consumers, such as mice and rabbits, eat plants which give them the energy to live and survive. Animals such as foxes and hawks are secondary consumers, because they gain energy by eating other animals. So energy flows through individual food chains (for example, the grass–rabbit–fox chain), making up a complex food web.

Caterpillars are primary consumers. They eat producers (plant leaves), and may be eaten by secondary consumers such as birds.

Carbon cycle

When animals eat plants, they 'burn' the food to release energy for growth and movement. At the same time they breathe carbon dioxide back into the air. Other plants then use the carbon dioxide to produce more food. This cycle keeps a natural balance of carbon dioxide and oxygen, as carbon moves to and from the Earth's atmosphere.

Like other animals, cows breathe out carbon dioxide. Their dung contains carbon, and in many parts of the world people burn it as fuel.

Ancient wood and fire

Wood was probably the first fuel ever used by humans. No one is sure when our prehistoric ancestors first used fire. It was certainly more than half a million years ago, and may have been inspired by a fire begun by a lightning bolt.

Humans seeing a fire started in this way might have tried rubbing sticks together or striking rocks to produce sparks and light their own fires. Fire brought great benefits. It was used for cooking, to provide warmth and light, and even to frighten animals away from shelters. Later, people learned to heat stones in the fire and drop them into a skin-lined pit of water to heat it. Gathering fuel became an important daily task, and the hearth was a key feature of prehistoric shelters. This early use of biomass material changed the way people lived.

This Spanish worker is burning wood in a pit to produce charcoal.

Charcoal

Thousands of years ago, people found that heaping wood into large piles or partly burying it before burning would make it smoulder slowly. This produced charcoal, which burns better than wood and makes less smoke. During the Iron Age in Europe, charcoal was used in furnaces for heating iron ore to temperatures high enough to release molten iron. The problem with using so much charcoal was the same as with wood – it meant chopping down trees and destroying forests.

The switch to coal

More than 2300 years ago, the ancient Greek philosopher Aristotle wrote about black rocks that looked like charcoal and burned well when they caught fire. He was referring to coal. By the 13th century, coal was being mined in northern Europe and it began to replace wood. Many people still preferred to burn wood in their homes, however, because they didn't like the smell of smoky, sooty coal.

FOSSIL FUELS

Coal, oil and natural gas are called fossil fuels, because they come from the fossilized remains of prehistoric plants and animals. They are buried biomass that formed millions of years ago and have to be mined from deep underground. When they are burned, fossil fuels release vast amounts of carbon dioxide into the atmosphere.

Coal was the essential fuel for steam locomotives. It boiled water and the resulting steam powered the engine. In the US, wood was mainly used to fire locomotives.

Energy crops

The best crops for bioenergy grow quickly and can be harvested easily every year. A tall, woody grass called Miscanthus, or elephant grass, is a good example. This grows very tall every year and can be cut down almost to the ground and then left to grow again for the next harvest.

Miscanthus is a dry grass which burns well and produces a great deal of energy. This type of grass came originally from China and Japan, but it grows well all over the world, in very different climates. Other grasses include bamboo and American switchgrass. Some trees also grow quickly and can be cut down to ground level before growing again, for example willow and poplar. Many of these plants are grown specifically for bioenergy and are called dedicated energy crops.

This worker is carrying a bundle of elephant grass across a river in Nepal.

A farmer uses a combine harvester to gather in his wheat crop. The waste straw can be used for bioenergy.

Multifunctional plants

Many plants can serve more than one purpose. Agricultural cereals, such as wheat, are mainly grown for food. The food comes from kernels at the head of the plant, which are ground into flour. This leaves the stems, or stalks, which can be bundled up as straw and used as biomass fuel. In the United States millions of tonnes of wheat straw are now used in this way, rather than being wasted.

Researchers are looking at ways of using sea plants to produce biofuels. Some seaweeds grow up to 20 metres in length every year, but they are difficult to harvest. Scientists at Tokyo University believe that large nets could be positioned off the coast of Japan, so that plants such as sea grape would grow on them and be harvested easily.

FOOD VERSUS FUEL

There is a shortage of food in many parts of the world, so some people feel that it is wrong to use food plants as fuel. Using waste parts of plants can help overcome this problem.

An underwater forest of kelp, a giant seaweed. Kelp is harvested for use as animal fodder and farm fertilizer, and can also be used for bioenergy.

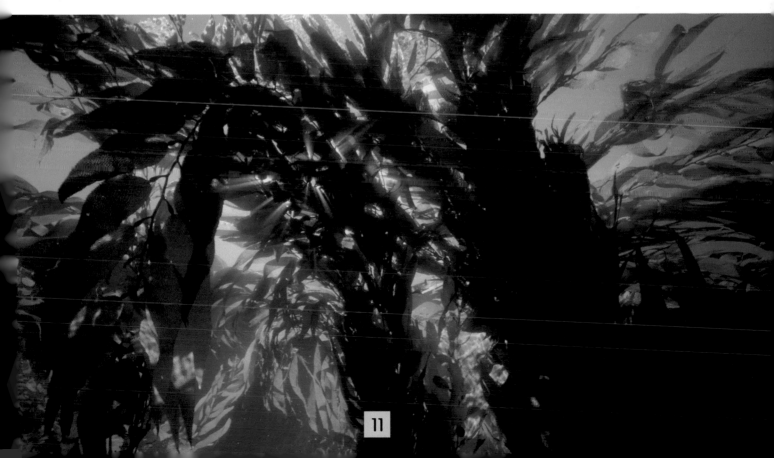

Burning biomass

We convert solid biomass into useful heat energy by burning it. When dry biomass reaches a temperature of 200°C or more, it gives off gases that mix with oxygen and burn. As the plant material burns, its carbon combines with the oxygen and is released as the gas carbon dioxide.

Scientists are concerned about this release because carbon dioxide is a greenhouse gas. This means that when it is released, it stays high in the atmosphere, soaking up and trapping heat from the Sun. However, the carbon dioxide released by

Wood can be recycled into chips and then used for pulp (to make paper) or as biomass material for burning.

These young people in Tanzania have walked many kilometres to bring back firewood for their families.

burning biomass is no greater than the amount that was taken in by the growing plants. Also, the carbon dioxide will be absorbed by the plants that grow in the burnt crop's place. This is called a closed carbon cycle and environmentalists call biomass a carbon-neutral resource. This means that it does not increase the overall amount of carbon dioxide in the atmosphere.

Wood for fuel

More than half the wood used in the world every year is burned as fuel. In many African countries, such as Kenya, Malawi and Tanzania, fuelwood is the major source of energy. In these countries many people spend a great deal of time every day searching for fuelwood. But burning wood in an open fire is not a very efficient way of using its energy. Aid agencies are introducing new kinds of stoves, so that fuelwood lasts longer and produces more heat.

Dry straw burns well and provides a good alternative to wood.

Straw-fired boilers

Because of a lack of wood, furnaces have been adapted to take materials such as straw. Furnaces in Denmark and other parts of Europe are powerful enough to take whole bales of straw. However, they are often backed up by oil- or gas-fired boilers, in case demand is high during the winter months. In Denmark, straw-fired furnaces are used to heat water for district heating systems.

Biofuels

Another way of using biomass as an energy source is to turn it into liquids called biofuels. The most important biofuel is ethanol (or bioethanol), which is a form of alcohol. This can be made from grasses such as sugar cane, maize and barley, or from vegetable plants such as sugar beet or potatoes.

The biofuel is produced by fermenting the plants, which means breaking them down chemically with yeast or a similar substance. This process is very similar to brewing beer, but the resulting ethanol is not suitable for drinking. It works very well as a fuel for cars. Scientists are also working on new ways of producing biofuels from wood and even waste paper. Interest is spreading across the world, as people look for ways to replace petrol, which is made from oil (a fossil fuel).

New storage tanks for ethanol were built at Brazil's largest port, Santos, in 2004. Biofuels have become an important export.

Replacing petrol

In 1975 the Brazilian government set up a national programme to introduce biofuels and use ethanol in cars. Brazil grows more sugar cane than any other country, so it makes sense to use it as a source of fuel. The programme has been a great success, and today most new Brazilian cars run on pure ethanol (also called E-100). Others use a mixture of ethanol and petrol, called gasohol.

Replacing diesel oil

Biodiesel is another way of using biomass as a fuel. It is produced by extracting oil from plants such as soya beans, rapeseed or peanuts. Small amounts can be produced with a simple press, and home-made biodiesel can even be made from recycled cooking oil. Like ethanol, it can be used neat (B-100), or it can be mixed with petroleum diesel. The most common blend is 20 per cent biodiesel (B-20).

VINE FUEL

In Sweden some new cars are running on E-85 fuel (85 per cent ethanol) made from vines from southern Europe. The biofuel is made instead of wine. Manufacturers say that the 15 per cent petrol content helps cars start better in very cold weather.

Biofuel is produced from wheat at this plant in France.

Using waste matter

Natural gas – the fossil fuel we find underground – is mainly methane. This gas forms when plants decay in places with no air. Bacteria and other microbes break down matter in plants at the bottom of ponds and marshes. That is why methane is also called marsh gas.

Methane from animal waste or wet plant matter can be collected and used as a fuel. This form is called biogas. The waste material is fed into a large metal tank, called a digester. After a couple of weeks, the biogas which has risen to the top of the digester is siphoned off through a pipe. The rest of the waste sinks to the bottom as a semi-liquid mass, or slurry, and is used as fertilizer by farmers.

The methane from this small biogas digester in India is used as a fuel for cooking.

Landfill sites

All over the world people throw away huge amounts of rubbish, including food waste, plant material and paper. Much of this waste is buried in landfill sites, which are simply giant holes in the ground. Over a period of time, the dumped refuse rots and releases a mixture of gases, mainly methane and carbon dioxide. Pipes can be buried in the waste, so that biogas is collected in a storage tank. It can then be burned in a power station to produce electricity.

Gasification

We can also convert solid biomass into a gas, using a process called gasification. Plant materials such as wood, rice husks or coconut shells can be heated to a high temperature without much oxygen in devices called reactors. The biomass gives off a mixture of gases, including methane, hydrogen and carbon monoxide. The gas can be used to produce electricity (see page 18).

(see page 18)

POWERFUL WASTE

One cubic metre of biogas (methane from waste) can produce enough power to light a 100-watt bulb for six hours, cook three meals for a family of six or drive a car 10–15 kilometres.

Every day we throw out tonnes of food waste. This can be used to make biogas.

Generating electricity

Recently scientists have found many new ways to generate electricity from biomass. The original method was to burn plant material (such as wood or paper waste) and use the heat created to boil water and create steam.

Just as in coal-fired power stations, the steam turns the blades of a turbine that is connected to an electric generator. Now gas turbines are replacing some steam turbines. These use hot gases to turn the blades directly. Some biogas power plants run on fresh sawdust, which burns in a furnace to produce the gas to drive the turbine. The hot gas is then used a second time, heating water to turn a steam turbine and produce more electricity.

This mountain of sawdust could be waste material. Or it could be used to make electricity.

Bagasse

When the juice has been removed from sugar cane to make sugar, a pulpy substance is left. This is called bagasse (from a Spanish word for pulp). This waste material makes good fuel. At Belle Vue, on the Indian Ocean island of Mauritius, a power station was built next to a sugar mill in 2000. For half the year, when enough bagasse is available, it is burned to power the steam turbines. For the rest of the time, the power station runs on coal imported from South Africa.

Turbines and generators

Inside a power plant, turbines and generators change mechanical energy into electrical energy. The mechanical energy may be the power of high-pressure steam or burning biogas, which turns the blades of a turbine connected by a shaft to a generator. Inside the generator, the shaft makes magnets spin inside wire coils to produce electricity. This technology was first used in 1831, when the British scientist Michael Faraday discovered that he could create electricity by moving a magnet through a coil of copper wire. The basic idea is still the same today and is used in all kinds of power stations.

Harvesting sugar cane in Mauritius. It can be used to make sugar and electricity.

Engineers work on the construction of a new gas turbine.

Source of hydrogen

Biomass can be used to produce the gas hydrogen. This is the simplest element in the universe. It combines with carbon to form petroleum and other so-called hydrocarbons. And it combines with oxygen to form water.

Hydrogen is not an energy source, because we always need energy to produce it, but it is a very useful carrier of energy. Most importantly, it can be used as a fuel to generate electricity. When biomass is gasified (see page 17), it gives off hydrogen, along with other gases such as methane. The hydrogen produced by biomass can be collected and then burned to produce heat or, even better, fed into a fuel cell to generate electricity.

A fuel cell powers a London taxi and produces no exhaust fumes.

Fuel cells

Fuel cells convert chemical energy to electrical energy. They generate electricity by combining hydrogen and oxygen, which then form water. Water is a harmless waste product, and this is one of the reasons why environmentalists are very keen on this technology. So long as it is supplied with the two gases, a fuel cell will go on supplying electricity. We have to make the hydrogen, and can use air as the source of oxygen.

Cars of the future?

Car manufacturers have developed cars specially for fuel-cell technology. There are still problems to be overcome. The technology is expensive, hydrogen is not easy to store, and the cells can be slow to warm up, which means that engine performance is not always good. Nevertheless, many experts believe that these will be the cars of the future.

This fuel-cell car drove all the way across Europe in 2004.

Around the world

Unlike fossil fuels and some other energy sources, biomass is produced all over the world. Experts calculate that one eighth of the biomass produced every year would be enough to satisfy the whole world's present demand for energy.

Overall, biomass provides about 13 per cent of the world's primary energy, with a small amount of this going towards making electricity. Biomass use as an energy source varies across the continents. For many people living in the world's developing countries, biomass – and especially wood – is the most important source of energy. The largest continent, Asia, is also the biggest user of biomass, followed by Africa and North America. Fuelwood alone provides nearly half of Africa's primary energy.

This woman in Ethiopia is cooking porridge on a metal stove.

These Indian girls are carrying dried cow dung that will be burned as fuel.

Power is in great demand during the Finnish winter months, when it is cold and dark.

Indian fuel

India uses more than 200 million tonnes of fuelwood every year – more than any other country. More than three quarters of the wood is used for cooking, and much of it does not come from forests but from farms, small plantations, and trees and shrubs along roads. Wood is also used as fuel in bakeries, brick and tile factories, and many small industries. In farming communities, dried animal dung – another form of biomass – is also burned as a fuel.

Finnish electricity

Finland is a country that produces electricity from many different sources. Fossil fuels (coal and gas), nuclear power stations and renewable sources all generate large amounts of power. The most important renewable source is hydropower (from hydroelectric dams), followed by biomass and wind power.

The Finns aim to produce half of their electricity from renewable sources by 2010. A power station in Lahti, north of the capital Helsinki, started producing electricity from oil-fired boilers in 1976, and changed to coal six years later. In 1998 the plant switched to using bark, wood chips and sawdust, and today it also uses household and industrial waste.

Renewable benefits

One of the greatest advantages of biomass power is that it is renewable. Many of the crops used for biomass grow and are harvested in a single year, and many renew themselves naturally.

Even specially planted trees, such as willow, can be harvested every three years. New shoots appear the following year, and the trees live for 30 years or more. New trees can then be planted. This cycle of growth and harvesting is very different from the one for fossil fuels, which take millions of years to form underground and then are mined rather than

This sewage plant produces methane, which is used for biomass power.

24

gathered in. Experts predict that reserves of coal will last little longer than 200 years, while oil and gas may run out in about 60 years' time. Yet most of today's electricity is still produced by power stations burning fossil fuels.

British landfill and sewage

Biomass is the most used renewable energy source in the UK, both for producing heat and generating electricity. Most biomass power comes from landfill gas, but there are many new developments. In 2001 a large sewage treatment works in the West Midlands, which serves 1.3 million people, began to use a system of digesters (see page 16). Now it produces enough electricity to run the whole plant. When the plant produces more power than it needs, it earns money by selling electricity to the national grid.

Australian eucalyptus

Most Australian energy, including electricity, is provided by coal. In fact, Australia exports more coal than any other country. But Australian interest in renewable energy is growing. In Western Australia, a company has been given permission to plant 12 million mallee trees, a fast-growing, bushy eucalyptus. The wood will fuel a biomass-fired power station, and the leaves will produce eucalyptus oil. The trees will also benefit the environment by helping to reduce the saltiness of the ground and preventing soil erosion.

These mallee shrubs and trees grow naturally in Australia.

Potential problems

Growing energy crops takes up a great deal of land, which can present a problem in some regions. This is especially true in countries that are short of water and where available agricultural land is used for growing food.

Environmentalists also worry that many biomass crops involve growing large amounts of one species (type) of plant in the same place. This can lead to an increase in pests and then pesticides, which can damage soil and the environment. Biomass materials need to be grown close to the place where they are to be used as fuel, because they are generally bulky. The harvested crop is often difficult and expensive to transport. Overall, however, experts agree that the advantages of biomass outweigh the disadvantages.

Harvesting a large crop of sugar cane on the Caribbean island of Martinique.

Deforestation

Where people use wood as fuel, they need to plant as many trees as they cut down. This has not been done in many countries, so whole forests have been cleared. This is called deforestation. In India, for example, less than one tenth of the enormous amount of fuelwood burned comes from sustained forests.

Global warming

Using biomass as fuel releases carbon dioxide, methane and other gases into the atmosphere. These greenhouse gases stay high in the atmosphere, soaking up and trapping heat from the Sun. This adds to problems of global warming, such as the melting of glaciers and polar icecaps. Though biomass causes fewer problems than fossil fuels, other renewable energy sources are even better.

Forests have been cleared in the Himalayan kingdom of Nepal. Today, much Nepalese biomass comes from farming waste – rice, maize, wheat and jute.

Future trends

Since biomass power is a renewable resource, we will probably use more of it in future. Experts agree that all renewable energy sources will become more important as the world's demand for energy continues to increase.

At the same time, people all over the world need to reduce their dependency on fossil fuels, because of the harm they cause to the environment. Biomass could be used to produce more electricity. At the moment it produces just a small amount, yet the demand for electricity is expected to nearly double during the next 25 years. We can all help to reduce this demand by using energy more wisely and sparingly.

The future belongs to renewable energy sources, such as wind and biomass.

Part of this CHP plant in Denmark is fired by burning straw. More biomass-fired plants will be built in future.

Combined heat and power

In Scandinavia and elsewhere, electric power stations are being converted so that they can also use biomass for heating systems. These combined heat and power (or CHP) plants use waste heat from turbines to heat nearby homes and factories. One CHP plant in Sweden also produces biomass pellets from sawdust, which are sold to other companies to use as fuel.

Small schemes

Renewable energy works well for local schemes. Many experts think biomass will become an important power source in poorer countries, as fuelwood becomes more scarce. In north-west India, more than 200 biogas digesters have been installed in villages around Ranthambhore National Park. Cow dung produces gas for cooking, reducing the need to gather wood and protecting an important wildlife reserve.

Using biogas helps to protect this natural habitat in India.

Glossary

bagasse A pulpy mass left after juice has been removed from sugar cane.

biodiesel A biofuel made from vegetable oil.

bioenergy Energy produced by biomass.

bioethanol A form of alcohol used as a biofuel.

biofuel A fuel produced by biomass.

biogas Gas fuel produced by biomass, especially methane.

biomass All plant and animal matter, especially when used as a fuel.

charcoal A black form of carbon made by heating wood.

CHP Short for combined heat and power, referring to a power station that produces electricity and useful heat.

compost A mixture of decayed plants and other organic matter.

continent One of the Earth's seven huge land masses.

decompose To decay or rot.

digester A tank in which biomass decomposes and produces biogas.

ecosystem A group of living things that are dependent on each other and their environment.

environmentalist A person who is concerned about and acts to protect the natural environment.

ferment To break (a substance) down chemically by the action of bacteria or yeast.

fossil fuel A fuel (such as coal, oil and natural gas) that comes from the remains of prehistoric plants and animals.

fuel cell A device that converts chemical energy into electricity.

fuelwood Wood used as fuel.

furnace An oven-like structure in which materials can be heated to very high temperatures.

gasification The process of converting solid or liquid biomass into a gas.

gasify To convert a solid or liquid into a gas.

gasohol A fuel made up of a mixture of ethanol and petrol (gasoline).

generator A machine that turns mechanical energy into electrical energy.

geothermal Produced by heat inside the Earth.

global warming The rise in temperature of the Earth's surface, especially caused by pollution from burning fossil fuels.

greenhouse gas A gas, such as carbon dioxide, that traps heat from the Sun in the atmosphere near the Earth and so helps to create a greenhouse effect.

habitat The natural home or environment of an animal or a plant.

hearth The place where a fire burns.

hydrocarbon A chemical compound containing hydrogen and carbon.

ore A rock or mineral containing a useful metal or valuable mineral.

petroleum Crude oil.

photosynthesis The process that plants use to make their own food from carbon dioxide, sunlight and water.

power station A plant where electricity is generated.

primary consumer An animal that eats only plants.

primary energy Energy that can be used directly or to make electricity.

secondary consumer An animal that eats other animals.

sewage Human waste matter.

slurry A semi-liquid mass of waste material.

terrarium A glass case holding a small ecosystem of plants and animals, with soil and air.

turbine A machine with rotating blades that turn a shaft.

Index